INSIDERS'GUIDE®

KID'S GUIDE SERIES

The Kid's Guide to Cruising Alaska

**Eileen Ogintz
with Reggie Yemma**

INSIDERS'GUIDE®

GUILFORD, CONNECTICUT
AN IMPRINT OF THE GLOBE PEQUOT PRESS

D1119791

About the Author

Eileen Ogintz writes the nationally syndicated column Taking the Kids, which appears in newspapers all over the country as well as on the Web. Reggie Yemma, Eileen's daughter, grew up in Connecticut and will be attending college in Colorado in September 2004. Reggie has helped her mom report on places that would be fun for kids since she was in elementary school. Their trips to Alaska are among their favorite family adventures.

INSIDERS'GUIDE ®

Copyright © 2004 by Eileen Ogintz

Text design: Eileen Hine
Map design: Stefanie Ward
Photo credits: Rubberball Productions: pp. i, 1, 13, 17, 23, 26, 32, 33, 43, 55, 56, 62, 63, 64, 69, 71, 73, 78, 79, 81, 87, 90, 97, 99. Photodisc: pp. 7, 38, 47.

Library of Congress Cataloging-in-Publication Data
Ogintz, Eileen
    The kid's guide to cruising Alaska / Eileen Ogintz with Reggie Yemma.– 1st ed.
        p. cm. – (Kid's guide series)
    ISBN 0-7627-3077-3
    1. Alaska–Guidebooks. 2. Ocean travel–Travel–Alaska–Guidebooks. 3. Cruise ships–Alaska–Guidebooks. 4. Children–Travel–Alaska Guidebooks. I. Yemma, Reggie.
II. Title. III. Series.
F902.3.O38 2004
917.9804'52–dc22

                                    2004047307

Manufactured in the United States of America
First Edition/First Printing

Contents

Acknowledgments

I want to thank all of the Alaskans—tourism experts, museum curators, town officials, National Park Service rangers, and parents—who gave freely of their time and knowledge to make sure we got their state "exactly right." I especially want to thank all of the Alaskan kids who offered their take on what visiting kids should know, and all of the visiting kids from "the Lower 48" who told us what was the most fun about their trips. Thanks also to the cruise lines for allowing us to ask their young guests about their Alaska experience and for answering my many questions about life aboard ship for passengers and crew. I hope every family who visits Alaska loves it as much as mine did. This project couldn't have been completed without the help of my favorite travelers: Andy, Matt, Melanie, and my hardworking co-author, Reggie. Thanks for always leading the way.

Travel SMarts

A lot of kids going on an Alaskan cruise fly to Vancouver or Seattle, where they start their cruise. It's a good idea to plan to entertain yourself while you're traveling. You also want to stay comfy, no matter what the weather, so make sure you've stashed a sweatshirt, fleece, or windbreaker in your backpack. You can also use all this stuff on the ship, in your cabin, and with your new friends:

— a CD player (and some favorite CDs), or an iPod or MP3 player.

— a book (a collection of jokes is always good)

— a deck of cards

— a water bottle and snacks

— your favorite handheld electronic games

— extra batteries

— disposable cameras

— blank notebook and crayons, markers, or pencils

— tape or a glue stick to paste in postcards along the way

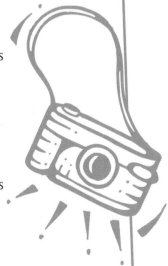

What else do you always bring on a trip?

CHAPTER 1

Welcome to Alaska

Welcome to Alaska! We hope this book makes your cruise even more fun. We've talked to a lot of kids your age about their experiences on Alaskan cruises, getting their advice on how to explore the ship and what adventures to seek out when you stop in port. We've asked about what there is to do on board and what you should bring.

Everyone agrees that there are two important things you need to bring on a cruise in Alaska: a camera to take pictures of all the beautiful scenery and—even more important—a sense of adventure! If you've never been on a cruise before, you probably have lots of questions about what you'll see and do on your journey. We hope this book answers them.

Your first question may be, "Where's all the snow?" Well, you won't see any in Anchorage in summer, or anywhere else except on the mountain peaks and the glaciers. In fact the weather probably will be a lot like Colorado or Vermont in early fall, with temperatures in the fifties and sixties.

Tip from a Cruising Kid

Don't go home without trying salmon and salmon jerky.

–EVAN, 12, Las Vegas, Nevada

You'll need a sweater or sweatshirt sometimes, but mostly it will be warm enough to go swimming. Don't forget your rain jacket—in the summer, it does rain a lot in southern Alaska, and that's where all of your cruise stops will be. Still, you'll have some perfect, sunny days too.

One thing you won't need is a flashlight. It never gets really dark in early summer. Because of the way the earth leans on its

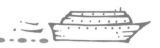

Web Sites

www.alaskazoo.org is the Web site for the zoo in Anchorage, where you can learn about many of Alaska's animals, like moose, bears, and reindeer.

www.alaskanative.net is the Web site for the Alaska Native History Center in Anchorage, where you can find out about native cultures.

www.anchorage.net is a good place to find out about what's fun to do in Anchorage.

www.imaginarium.org is the Web site for Alaska's only hands-on science center. It's in Anchorage.

www.anchoragemuseum.org is the Web site for the Anchorage Museum of History and Art, where you can find out about Alaskan history and village life. Check out their kids corner.

www.travelalaska.com is a good Web site to help plan your trip.

www.h2oasiswaterpark.com is the Web site for a fun indoor water park in Anchorage.

axis toward the sun in summer, and because Alaska is so far north, sometimes it can stay light for more than eighteen hours a day.

You're probably starting your Alaskan adventure in **Anchorage,** Alaska's biggest city. But don't be in too much of a hurry to get on the ship: You'll want to see Anchorage's many attractions. Anchorage is on the Pacific Ocean's Cook Inlet. It's named after Captain James Cook, who came here in 1778.

On a clear day you should be able to see six mountain ranges from Anchorage. Want to try?

- Talkeetna Mountains to the north
- Chugach Mountains to the east
- Kenai Mountains to the south
- Tordrillo to the west
- Aleutian Range to the southwest
- And, of course, to the north, if you're lucky and the clouds are thin, Mount McKinley and the Alaska Range

More than half of all the people who live in Alaska live in Anchorage. It has a population of 250,000. Anchorage seems more like a town than a bustling city. You might even see a moose in a neighborhood, a bear downtown, a whale in the water, or a Dall sheep in the cliffs near the highway! Watch for bald eagles too. See if you can spot them hunting along the tidal areas, looking for fish.

Speaking of animals, check out the **Alaska Zoo** while you're in Anchorage. You can see all kinds of animals that live in the Alaska wilderness: black bears, brown bears, a polar bear, and, of course, reindeer. Make sure to see the statue of **Star the Reindeer.**

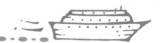

Stop in at the **Alaska Public Lands Information Center** downtown on West 4th Avenue, where National Park Service rangers can answer all of your questions about where to go hiking, kayaking, or fishing. If you're lucky, the day you visit will be a special Kids Day at the center. These are held from time to time in the summer. On a Kids Day, the rangers tell stories about Alaskan animals, put on puppet shows, and sometimes have animals visit from the Alaska Zoo.

In summer kids who live in Anchorage spend as much time as they can outdoors. There are more than 200 parks here, and all along the Coastal Trail, you'll see parents and kids out biking and in-line skating. You also can find hiking trails that begin in the city or nearby in Chugach State Park.

Go check out the floatplanes at **Lake Hood.** These are small planes that look like they have water skis on the bottom and can land in water. For many people in Alaska, floatplanes are their favorite form of transportation. Lake Hood is the busiest floatplane lake anywhere. Maybe your family will take a floatplane ride while you're in Alaska to see a glacier or Mount McKinley. Other people take the planes to get to remote places to fish.

Anchorage's **Imaginarium Science Center** in the heart of downtown is a place where you can hold a sea star from an Alaska tide pool, look through the eyes of a grasshopper, or stand inside a giant bubble. It's a great bet for a rainy day.

Make sure to leave time for the **Alaska Native Heritage Center**. Here's your chance to learn about members of Alaska's eleven cultural groups—they speak twenty different languages!—and find out about their cultures. To make it easier, the center is organized around these five cultural groups:

- **The Athabascans:** They traditionally moved a lot from place to place to hunt and fish.

- **The Yup'Ik and Cup'Ik:** In the old days all the men and boys old enough to leave their moms lived together in a house while girls and women lived in smaller houses.

- **Inupiaq and Saint Lawrence Island Yupik Eskimos:** They used boats big enough to carry fifteen people—and a ton of cargo.

- **The Aleut and Alutiiq:** These tribes lived in southern Alaska, in villages where life revolved around the water and fishing.

- **The Eyak, Tlingit, Haida, and Tsimshian:** They lived in southeastern Alaska and traditionally traveled everywhere by canoe. They built their villages within easy access to river streams and the ocean.

At the center you can meet tribal members of all ages. There are performances of traditional dances, songs, and stories. You can also walk through traditional houses where tribe members will greet you and show you how native crafts are made.

You can find out more about Alaska at the **Anchorage Museum of History and Art,** downtown. Ask for a special "Family Guide" brochure, then go time traveling through thousands of years in the Alaska Gallery on the museum's second floor. There are dioramas about what life was like in Alaska long ago, from

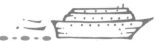

native tribes to those adventurous folks who came during the Gold Rush. The masks are really cool, and so is the just-for-kids area in the museum. The museum even has a kids area on its Web site, which has fun games and activities based on what's going on in the museum.

Mush!

If you think Anchorage is busy now, come during the first week in March. That's when people gather from around the world for the start of the Iditarod sled dog race. The word *Iditarod* comes from an Indian word that means "the distant place." The mushers race from Anchorage to Nome, more than 1,100 miles. That's as far as from New York to Dallas. Each musher races twelve to sixteen dogs that can run as fast as fourteen miles per hour—100 miles a day! The race honors the brave men who took their sled dogs to Nome in 1925 to bring life-saving medicine during a diphtheria outbreak. Kids fourteen and older can race their own teams in the 160-mile-long Junior Iditarod held the week before the main race.

Many Alaskans use dog sleds to travel all winter. They take very good care of their dogs, sometimes even feeding their animals before they themselves eat, or giving their dogs water before they take a drink. If you were here in the winter, you'd see people running their dogs every weekend on local trails. There is a special area on the Iditarod Web site (www.iditarod.com) for kids. You may get a chance to drive a dog sled team while you're in Alaska, but you'll have to go up on the Juneau Icefield or near Skagway, on the Denver Glacier. Many families want to take these trips, even though they're expensive. Your cruise ship will have information about these trips and many other adventures. Ask your parents to book ahead—before you get to Alaska.

The Pipeline

Headquartered in Anchorage, the Alyeska Pipeline Service Company built and maintains the Trans-Alaska oil pipeline. It begins at Prudhoe Bay on the Artic Coast and stretches 800 miles southwest across Alaska to the port town of Valdez. It carries crude oil over three mountain ranges, more than thirty rivers, and many creeks. Since it was built in the 1970s, the pipeline has carried billions of gallons of oil. Everyone who lives in Alaska—kids too—gets an annual "royalty" check from the state. The money is earned from selling the oil.

"Seward's Ice Box"

In 1867 U.S. Secretary of State William Seward bought Alaska for $7.2 million from the Russians who controlled the territory. Most Americans thought buying Alaska was a big mistake. They believed the Russians had taken everything valuable

DID YOU KNOW?

The natives named this place *Alyeska,* or "where the weather comes from." Alaska became the forty-ninth state on January 3, 1959. More than twice the size of Texas, it's not only the biggest state: It has three million lakes and more coastline than the rest of the continental U.S.

DID YOU KNOW?

A thirteen-year-old boy designed Alaska's flag in 1926. Benny Benson drew the seven stars of the Big Dipper and the North Star in gold on a dark blue background and his design won a contest. Many years later, when Alaska became a state, his flag became the state flag.

DID YOU KNOW?

There's no true night in late spring or early summer in Alaska, only a short period of twilight after 11:00 P.M. before the sun rises again. Try asking your parents if you can stay up until it gets dark!

DID YOU KNOW?

During extremely cold winter nights, a lot of Alaskans plug their cars engine heaters into electric outlets to keep them warm. That way they can be sure the cars will start in the morning.

DID YOU KNOW?

Alaska's Dall sheep come down from the cliffs to graze by the side of the road along the Seward Highway. You should be able to spot them up in the cliffs if you look hard enough. The males have huge horns that curl into circles and the females have shorter ones. They live in the rocky cliffs because it's harder for predators to get at them.

before they left. But Alaska turned out to be one of the greatest deals Americans ever made because of all of its natural resources, wildlife, and beauty.

Kenai Fjords National Park

Before you board your ship, you can take a tour boat from **Seward,** through Resurrection Bay, a great place to spot sea life. (Seward is a beautiful community about 126 miles south of Anchorage.) Did you see any whales? How many different animals did you see? The fjords are tall, glacier-carved valleys that are now filled with ocean water. There's also a 35-mile-long ice field in the park. Exit Glacier is the only part of the park that you can walk to from the road, but you will see the glacier from a boat too. Many people like to kayak in the park and there are trips offered. Stop in at the visitor center in Seward where National Park Service rangers can answer all your questions. If you're lucky, you might even see the ice crack and hear it groan, kind of like a giant creak, followed by a loud crash.

An Alaskan Kid Says

The light summer nights are great for late night games of basketball. We just have to be careful we don't lose track of the time!

–ELIZABETH, 16, Anchorage

Sea Life in Seward

Speaking of Seward, scientists at the SeaLife Center in Seward are working hard to figure out how to keep Stellar sea lions, an endangered species, healthy. In fact they've just brought some sea lion babies to live at the center. You can see the sea lions in a huge tank that was built to be just like the waters around Seward, where many sea animals live. Researchers here also use remote-control cameras to monitor sea lions living miles away. Say "hi" to the harbor seals while you're at it, and the sea birds.

At the Discovery Pool, reach in and touch sea stars, sea urchins, sea cucumbers, and other creatures. You can look into the window of one of the center's labs, where the researchers are working. There is also a rescue team that helps injured and stranded animals: seals, whales, sea otters, and birds. Here's your chance to learn all about Alaskan sea life.

Check off what you saw:

   — sea lion   — puffin   — harbor seal

   — giant squid   — kelp

Oil Spill

On March 24, 1989, in Prince William Sound, a supertanker named the *Exxon Valdez* crashed into a rock and got a hole in its side, spilling most of its cargo—11 million gallons of oil. It was the worst oil spill in U.S. history. More than 250,000 marine birds, mammals, and fish died from the sticky, black oil. Because the oil got into their fur and feathers, the animals couldn't stay warm, and some died from the cold. They were also poisoned by eating the oil. Nearly 1,500 miles of Alaska's shoreline were damaged. Many fishermen lost their jobs. It took more than 4 summers, 10,000 workers, about 1,000 boats, and roughly 100 airplanes and helicopters to clean up the spill. In addition, over time, the wave action from winter storms scoured the beaches clean. Today, you won't see any oil polluting Prince William Sound, but the sea life still hasn't fully recovered. The Exxon company said it spent more than $2 billion on the cleanup. Some of that money helped establish the Seward SeaLife Center.

An Alaskan Kid Says

We're just like kids from the Lower 48 except that it's not that hot and the lighting is different. We have different wildlife and terrain. About two weeks ago, a moose and her calf walked right through our yard.

–SPENCER, 12, Girdwood

Museum Smarts in Alaska

When you're visiting a museum, make sure you've got water, snacks, and comfy shoes.

Bring along a pad and pencil so you can sketch your favorite painting.

Get some postcards at the entrance showing the museum's paintings, sculptures, and masks, then "hunt" for them as you tour the museum.

CHAPTER 2

Welcome Aboard!

Finally! You're here . . . on board the ship. All those months of planning . . . that long plane ride . . . and now you're really here!

Get ready to be treated like a VIP (Very Important Person). See how the whole crew—and there are many of them—are smiling at you as you board the ship. Everyone wants you to have a good time.

The ship is big. Think of it as a floating hotel. Or even a small town on water. There are restaurants and swimming pools, movie theaters and libraries, Internet cafes and musical theaters.

You'll notice that people on board are from all over the world. It's not uncommon for the crew to come from more than a dozen different countries, including Canada, England, the Philippines, and Jamaica.

Web Sites

www.state.ak.us/kids is the special kid's area of the state of Alaska Web site. Here you can learn fun facts, take virtual tours, and lots more!

www3.telus.net/cruise_watch/alaska.htm is a site from a cruising fan with lots of pictures of cruise ships, ship itineraries, and info and links on cruising Alaska.

You can also visit the Web site for your own cruise line and find out more about the ship you're going to call home. Ask your parents for the Web address.

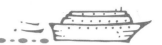

Many of the crew are in white uniforms. They have all different jobs, from mopping the deck to serving drinks to figuring out the ship's route. The captain is the boss. You'll probably hear him on the loudspeakers making announcements.

The first thing you need to do is find the room where you will be staying. It is called a stateroom or cabin on board a cruise ship. It's probably smaller than your room at home, but it's so cozy. Does your bed fold down from the wall at night? You may even discover an animal made from a towel waiting for you when you go to bed. Ask your steward—the person who takes care of your cabin—if he or she will show you how to make a monkey or a duck.

Every night, your steward will leave you a schedule of the next day's activities—especially for your age group—at the ship's kids club. You can be busy from morning until late at night. You'll probably be able to take your pick of activities. Ice painting, Lego building, making friendship bracelets. Scavenger hunts, game nights, karaoke. Talent shows, computer games, arcade games. It's almost like camp. You'll even have counselors who will plan activities to help you learn more about Alaska.

The counselors will also help you to meet some of the other kids, especially if you're shy. They're really good at getting everybody involved in the fun stuff, as long as you show up at the kids club area on the ship. Every cruise line has different names for their activities for kids, and they

Tip from a Cruising Kid

Go up and talk to people and ask their name. The best way to make friends on the ship is to talk to people and get to know them.

—EMILIE, 10, Detroit, Michigan

usually have different clubs for kids of different ages. You'll probably meet some of the counselors as soon as you board. They'll say "hi" as you walk up the gangway and tell you what they've got planned for your first night on board. As soon as you find your stateroom, you'll probably want to find the kids area on your ship for your age group. A lot of times it's on one of the top decks, near the pool and the arcade. And the counselors usually have an "open house" the first afternoon or night of the cruise.

Check out what you can do with your family—shows at night, basketball, shuffleboard, Ping-Pong. There are pools and hot tubs for everyone to enjoy. Now's the time to get your grandpa or some other adult to teach you to play poker. Some ships even have climbing walls, minigolf, and in-line skating.

What do you think your favorite thing to do on board will be?

Write Down Something You Did Today That You Never Did Before:

_____

_____

_____

_____

_____

_____

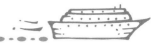

You'll never be hungry on board. Even better, here's your chance to try new foods as well as load up on your favorites. You can order whatever you want in the dining room—even three desserts (if your parents let you) or four burgers! There's no extra charge, no matter how much you eat. Your parents will have to pay for the drinks you order outside the dining room, however. So ask your parents about purchasing a drink card to cover all of your soft drinks. No matter what time of day it is, you can always find something to eat—pizza, ice cream, cookies, sandwiches, fruit, and other treats. And you can order room service for free. Some kids like to order a snack when they get back from exploring on land when the ship stops in different towns. Some ships have a giant late-night buffet. You might want to stay up and go even if you're not hungry, just to see all the ice sculptures, and chocolate desserts.

Write Down a New Food—Something You Ate That You Never Had Before:

_____

_____

_____

_____

Are you one of those kids who likes to go to the kids clubs just so you can hang out with your friends—and be without your mom and dad? The clubs are open at night so you can eat dinner with your family and then meet up with other kids.

Even though the ship is big, you'll have it figured out in a day or so. **Quick tip:** A lot of times it's faster to go up and down the stairs than to wait for the elevators.

Another tip: If you're really hungry in the morning, go to the buffet where you can get all kinds of food, fast. Waffles anybody?

Whatever you do on board ship, don't spend all your time indoors. There's too much too see, like glaciers or maybe even whales. Some lucky cruisers will get to see dolphins jumping. Have you seen any animals today? Don't worry if it rains. Just put on your rain jacket and wave to the whales!

The towns and cities where the ship stops are called ports. And you can be sure that your time off the ship will be just as busy as your time on board. You and your family will be exploring little towns, shopping, kayaking or fishing, riding trains and helicop-

ters, maybe even dog sledding. It'd be great if everyone in your family took turns picking what you do off the ship. Go along with what the rest of the family wants to do, and they'll be more willing to do what you like.

Put Your Picture of the Ship Here
And write down what you like about your stateroom.

DID YOU KNOW?

More than 750,000 people come to Alaska every summer on cruise ships. That includes thousands of kids. How many kids are on your ship? Where do they come from? List five of their hometowns:

1. _____

2. _____

3. _____

4. _____

5. _____

DID YOU KNOW?

There are 4,800 hamburgers and 22,300 cans of soda used on one big ship in one week. The ship's 2,100 passengers also eat 32,000 eggs and 5,320 bananas!

DID YOU KNOW?

Sea otters are really smart. They put shellfish on their chests and crack them with rocks! Watch them playing along the shoreline. There are now more than 150,000 sea otters in Alaska.

DID YOU KNOW?

Female Steller sea lions grow up to be eleven feet long and weigh 2,200 pounds. Males may get even bigger!

New Friends

Look around. Depending on the size of the ship, there may be 300 or more kids on board. Don't be shy. Here's your chance to make some new friends—fast. The best way is to go to some of the organized kids activities the first night and

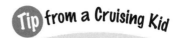

next day on board. The counselors will help you get to know other kids—and you'll have a lot of fun playing games, listening to music, or watching movies in the special kids areas on the ship. *The good news:* Once you make a few friends, you won't ever be bored because there will be so much to do, even at night. Here's your chance to get your mom and dad to let you stay up late. It's vacation, after all! The counselors are really cool too. So don't spend all your time hanging around your stateroom.

Scavenger Hunt

Team up with a brother, sister, friend, or even go solo to find the most essential parts of your ship, then check them off below!

— The bridge (*Hint:* where the captain and his officers often work)

— An indoor swimming pool

— The arcade

— The bow (front) of the boat

— Minigolf, basketball, or Ping-Pong courts

___ The muster station

___ A souvenir shop

___ The stern (back) of the boat

___ The kids club

___ The fancy dining hall

___ The place to get ice cream

___ The place to get pizza, burgers, or hot dogs

Lifeboat Drill

One of the first things you'll do after boarding the ship is a "lifeboat drill." In each stateroom guests will find life jackets. Each jacket is labeled with the number of a specific muster station. A muster station is where you go to board lifeboats if it's ever necessary. The path to the muster station is mapped out on a sign on the back of your stateroom door. When the ship's captain sounds the emergency horn, signaling the start of the muster drill, your family must put on its life jackets and report to its muster station. At the muster station, you will be checked off a roll call list. The captain will give some additional information on the ship rules and then send you on your way. You won't get to climb into the lifeboats, but you'll know where they are, just in case. Chances are you will never have to use a lifeboat.

Tip from a Cruising Kid

The thing that surprised me most on the ship was that the food was free.

–LUKE, 11, Madison, Wisconsin

CHAPTER 3

Glaciers Everywhere

One of the most exciting things about Alaska is the glaciers, and you'll be seeing plenty of them as you cruise through **Glacier Bay.** Just keep a look out for what looks like gigantic icebergs or snow banks passing by the side of the ship. The glaciers you're seeing are real live evidence of the last ice age, 20,000 years ago, when most of the earth was covered in ice. Some glaciers have been here for thousands upon thousands of years.

It's hard to believe that the bay you are cruising through now was not much more than a dent in a gigantic wall of ice only 300 years ago. In 1794 the English explorer Captain George Vancouver sailed through something called the Icy Straight of Southeast Alaska looking for a passage to Europe. Instead of finding Europe, he found a wall of ice 20 miles wide and 4,000 feet thick. Almost one hundred years later, in 1879, California biologist John Muir decided to give the Icy Straight another try. But when Muir arrived, the giant ice wall was nowhere in sight. It had moved back more than 40 miles, forming the bay your ship will be cruising through.

Web Site

www.nps.gov/webrangers. A cool Web site for kids about national parks.
Click on the map of Alaska.

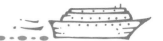

The wall of ice that Captain Vancouver encountered was a glacier, just like the ones you see. A glacier forms when snow falls faster than it melts for years at a time. In Alaska this happens because the temperature, especially in the winter, can be very cold. Snow will fall, and before *that* layer has time to melt, more snow will fall, and before that layer has time to melt . . . you get the idea. Eventually, so many heavy layers of snow pile on top of each other that the ones on the bottom are squashed into very thick ice that melts extremely, extremely slowly (if at all). This is why glaciers seem to never melt.

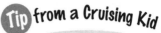

The things that surprised me the most on the ship were the glaciers! Keep your camera out so you can take pictures of them.

–ASHLEY, 11, Washington, D.C.

Actually, they are melting, just very, very slowly. Because glaciers are so gigantic, and because more layers of snow are added to them every year, they rarely disappear.

Glaciers are a lot like the layers of a cake . . . but not a very tasty one. The top layer is made of soft, freshly fallen snow. The next layer down is old, more densely packed snow. Then the next layer down is even older, compacted snow, called "firn." And, finally the bottom layer is the base, which is made of dense, clear ice.

Alaska is filled with glaciers. There are more than 750 lakes that have a glacier at one end or another, and three-quarters of the fresh water in Alaska is stored as glacial ice—more than all the water in the lakes, ponds, and rivers in all of the Lower 48. Five percent of the entire state of Alaska is covered in glaciers. That would be like the entire state of South Carolina covered in ice.

Another thing that makes glaciers special is that they keep moving, even when they are so huge!

Glaciers can move two different ways: They can advance (move forward), or they can recede (move back). They usually move down mountain valleys or out across plains. Then they eventually settle into the sea, where they're called icebergs.

An Alaskan Kid Says

Watch for a glacier from the towns you visit. A lot of times you can see one.

–HANNAH, 7, Skagway

The Alaskan landscape is shaped from glaciers advancing and retreating. The huge glaciers act as a push broom as they move, carrying rocks and debris far from their original home and moving the landscape around. That's why the ice often looks dirty. Glacial movement is responsible for many of Alaska's U-shaped valleys, steep walled basins, and hanging valleys. Just imagine a huge glacier plowing through the view in front of you, forming everything you see.

Welcome to the Inside Passage

Can you trace the route your ship is taking? Are you going north to south or south to north? If you are having trouble figuring this out, ask the activities director to help you map your trip.

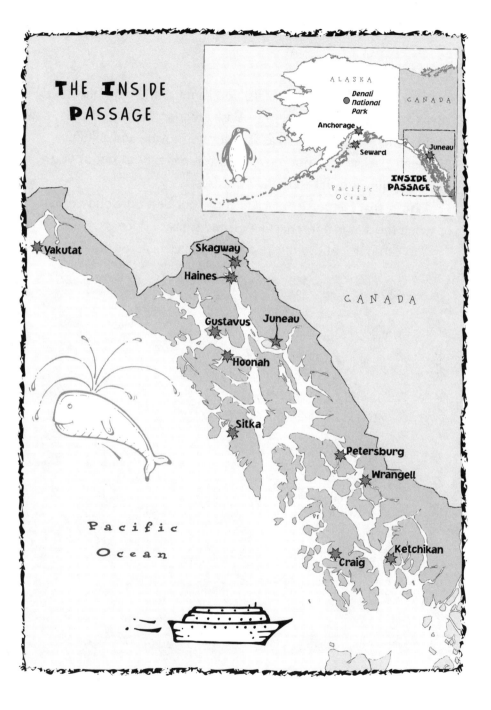

THE INSIDE PASSAGE

ALASKA

CANADA

Denali National Park

Anchorage

Seward

Juneau

INSIDE PASSAGE

Pacific Ocean

Yakutat

Skagway

Haines

CANADA

Gustavus

Juneau

Hoonah

Sitka

Petersburg

Wrangell

Pacific

Ocean

Craig

Ketchikan

Ice Moves

If you want to find active glaciers, you came to the right place. There are more active glaciers in Alaska than in the rest of the world. When a glacier is active, it is always moving and shifting. Although glaciers may not move as fast as a car, or as fast as you can walk, they are still constantly moving.

Photo tip: Pictures of glaciers come out best on cloudy days or when the sun is not reflecting off the snow and ice.

You can put a photo of the coolest glacier here, or draw one!

Birds of the Bay

There are more than 230 species, or different types, of birds that live in Glacier Bay. Here is a checklist of the most common birds in the bay. Which have you seen? Which have you heard of?

— bald eagle

— rufous hummingbird

— ruby-crowned kinglet

— hermit thrush

— chestnut-backed chickadee

— blue grouse

— hairy woodpecker

— black-legged kittiwake

— tufted puffin

— pelagic cormorant

— pigeon guillemot

— arctic tern

— black oystercatcher

Ranger Work

Imagine having a job that lets you hang out with bears, whales, and bald eagles almost every day. How cool would that be? Well that is what the National Park Service rangers in Glacier Bay get to do. They protect and take care of the Glacier Bay National Park.

They also teach people how special national parks, and the wildlife in them, are. They enforce important rules in the bay, such as not feeding the animals or not picking wildflowers, so that fifty years from now kids just like you will be able to enjoy the same places. They also build trails that give the people visiting the park a place to walk without trampling the wildlife or animal shelters, so the plants and animals are protected.

Park rangers work hard to make Alaska extra special for kids, and you could become a "Junior Ranger" or even a "Teen

???

DID YOU KNOW?

There are four different types of glaciers in Alaska:

Cirque glaciers: These are small glaciers that occupy small hollows in the mountains.

Piedmont glaciers: These glaciers form at the base of very steep mountains.

Alpine glaciers: These glaciers form within mountain ranges, generally around the top.

Valley glaciers: These glaciers flow through low valleys.

DID YOU KNOW?

It took thousands of years for Glacier Bay to fill with ice, but just 200 years for it to melt!

DID YOU KNOW?

Many Alaskans chip off pieces of floating icebergs to use for ice in their drinks. Compressed air trapped in the ice makes the bubbles burst with a snap, crackle, and pop. Alaskan kids call this "ice sizzle."

Explorer." Often, park rangers come aboard the ship to talk to kids when you're cruising through Glacier Bay. Just ask the first park ranger you see and he or she will be glad to help you. You'll soon need to make room on your backpack or sweatshirt for a shiny new "Junior Ranger" badge!

Glaciers Up Close

If you think looking at glaciers is cool, try walking on one! You can trek through the snow, and maybe even drink glacier water from a spring. There are plenty of activities to do on glaciers that are especially for cruise passengers—dog sledding, glacier trekking, and helicopter tours, so you get to see the glaciers up close. Tell your parents which things you think would be the most fun, and they'll help you sign up. Don't forget your sunglasses, because it's really bright on the snow. Bring mittens too.

Do You See Blue?

When you look at one of the glaciers you cruise by, do you notice anything odd about it? What color is it? It looks blue, even though snow is white. Weird! That's because the ice molecules of the glaciers are able to absorb all colors of the spectrum except the color blue. That's why glaciers look blue.

Calving

Listen for loud cracks and booms. It's not thunder. It's the glaciers doing something called *calving*. That means a piece of the glacier is breaking off and falling into the water, forming an iceberg of its own. Calving happens because gravity draws the glacier ice down the mountains. When the ice hits the water, it melts, causing a piece of the glacier to collapse into the water. This happens a few times an hour, so keep your ears open and your eyes peeled!

CHAPTER 4

Bears, Whales, and Salmon! Alaskan Wildlife

Get ready to talk to the animals. Not really, but on this trip you'll see more animals than you'll ever see anyplace else in the wild: bears, whales, salmon, sea otters, bald eagles, moose, and many more. Everyone who comes to Alaska wants to see the amazing wildlife. You will too!

Three species of bears call Alaska home; there are black bears, grizzly bears, and even some polar bears way up in the Arctic region of Alaska. Black bears are the smallest of the three. They usually weigh between 200 and 300 pounds, but some grow to be as big as 500 pounds. The bears between 200 and 300 pounds are about as heavy and as large as a washing machine, and the 500-pound bears are about as heavy and as large as a refrigerator. That is big! Black bears have pretty poor eyesight, so they have to depend on their sense of smell—which is very sharp—to help them find food. Black bears are also omnivorous, which means that they eat any type of food that they can find. But they usually end up eating plants because they have a hard time finding meat or fish. Black bears are found mostly in southeastern Alaska, around Prince William Sound, and in the coastal mountains and lowlands of south-central Alaska.

Web Sites

www.nationalgeographic.com/kids/ is a special Web site just for kids that will tell you lots about animals and the outdoors, with planty of fun games and facts.

www.nps.gov is the Web site for all of the national parks. You can link to any of the parks you think you'll be visiting in Alaska to figure out what to do when you get there!

www.alaskaseafood.org gives lots of info on Alaska salmon and other fish. The site also has recipes you can try after you catch one!

www.alaskascenes.com/wildlife is packed with photos taken by Alaskans of animals you may get to see when you visit.

You can probably consider grizzly bears—also known as brown bears—to be the big brothers of black bears, because most grizzlies are anywhere from twice to three or four times the size of black bears. Adult grizzlies can weigh over 1,000 pounds, which is about as much as a race car weighs. Grizzlies also have a distinct shoulder hump, which sets them apart from black bears. Just like black bears, grizzlies eat all the plants and animals that they can get their paws on. But grizzlies have an easier time finding meat and fish. Because of their size, they are at the top of the food chain, making many other animals fear them. Grizzlies live all over Alaska. The search for food keeps them on the move. The third kind of bear, the polar bear, lives in the Arctic near the coast, so chances are you'll only see one in a zoo.

Whales

Whales swim in all the seas around Alaska. Even though whales live in the water, they are mammals just like we are. Altogether, there are at least four-teen species of whales found in the waters around the state. But all whales are one of two different types: *toothed whales* or *baleen whales*. Do you know what the difference is? Well, clearly toothed whales have teeth. Some whales that live in Alaska and fall under this category would be sperm whales, belugas, orcas, pilot whales, beak whales, dolphins, and porpoises. A *baleen* is a sort of fringed screen that hangs down in a whale's mouth instead of teeth—this also gives baleen whales their name. Baleen helps these whales catch and eat their food. Some baleen whales that can be found in Alaska are blues, bowheads, northern rights, fin-backs, humpbacks, seis, and minkes.

So keep a sharp lookout for the unique wildlife, and watch for groups of whales swimming through the waters or pink salmon leaping into the air. See if there are any eagles soaring through the sky or sea otters floating through the water on their backs. There might even be a bear eating a piece of fish on the shore. Just keep your eyes wide open!

An Alaskan Kid Says

We don't ride polar bears and we don't dog mush everywhere!

−BRETT SWANSON, 13, via e-mail

Whale Talk

Whales are considered very vocal mammals; they make just about as much noise under the water as we humans do on land. But if we heard the whales talking, we would not quite understand what

they were saying. Whale language is a mixture of grunts, clicks, chirps, whistles, squeaks, and even shrill calls. Whales use these sounds to help them communicate as well as find their food.

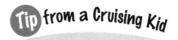
The areas where whales usually look for food are often dark and murky, places very hard for them to navigate with just their eyesight. So whales use a type of "sonar." They make a series of sounds, and these sound waves hit fish and echo back to the whales. The whales use the echoes to figure out the distance, shape, and texture of the fish near them.

Fishing Alaskan Style

You may get to go fishing when you're in Alaska. Probably you'll go with your parents and a guide. Make sure to follow directions. It's hard to get the fish on the hook. If you go fishing remember:

- Hold onto the rod when you get a fish. Fish here are bigger than those you might be used to. Halibut can weigh more than you do—over one hundred pounds. Salmon can be as heavy as fourteen pounds.

- Pay attention to where you've got your pole. You don't want to swing your pole and catch someone (or yourself) with your hook.

- Bring extra socks and extra layers of clothes. It can get very chilly out on the water. A hat and mittens are a good idea too.

- Bring your favorite snacks. You're going to get hungry!

- Be careful on the riverbanks. It's slippery. That's also why it's a good idea to wear a life vest on any fishing excursion.

- There are so many fish in the rivers here that you are bound to catch at least one—the question is, what type?

Bear Watching

A trip to Alaska is definitely not complete without at least one bear sighting. There are a lot of parks where you might see as many as three bears at a time! Admiralty Island, about 10 miles west of Juneau, is a great place to see brown bears. So, when you visit, make sure to have your camera ready. But remember to follow the rules at the viewing site and stay at least 100 yards (about the length of a football field without the goalposts) away from any bears.

The National Park Service says: Avoid surprise encounters. Make noise to let bears know you are coming— sing and shout as you walk. Avoid whistling or grunting (a bear may think you're food or a threat). Chances are, a bear won't come near you. A park ranger or guide can give you more "bear aware" advice.

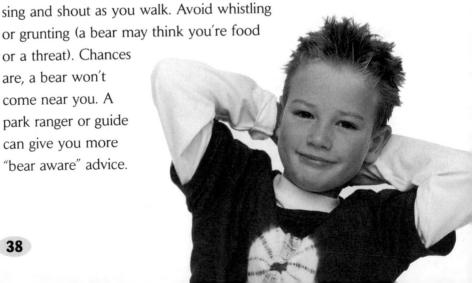

Salmon or Salmon?

Most native Alaskans know the difference between the five types of salmon that live in Alaska. Here are some facts you can use to strike up a conversation with your fishing guide.

- **Chinook salmon:** This salmon's nickname is "king salmon." It is the Alaska state fish and it is bluish green on its back with a white belly.

- **Chum salmon:** This salmon's nickname is "dog salmon" because they are fed to sled dogs. They are a metallic green on their backs and silver on their bellies.

- **Coho salmon:** The coho's nickname is "silver salmon." This is because they are bright orange. Just kidding! They're silver.

- **Pink salmon:** This salmon is pink, just like its name, but it also has the nickname of "humpback salmon" because the males, once they are full grown, grow a hump in their backs.

- **Sockeye salmon:** Sockeye salmon are also called "red salmon" because they turn a very bright red once they spawn, or lay their eggs.

You Otter Know This!

Sea otters are often seen along the seashores of Alaska. They are so cute and furry, and keeping their fur clean is one of their most important pastimes. Sea otters are the only marine mammals that do not have a layer of fat to keep them warm. Instead, they have very, very thick coats, which they depend on for warmth. In fact sea otters have the thickest fur of any animal in the world!

Because the fur is so thick, millions of tiny air bubbles are trapped inside, which helps keep the otters warm in the freezing waters of Alaska. These air bubbles also help them float on top of the water. But if the otters do not groom, their fur will become too matted to hold the air bubbles. Then cold water can slip through and freeze them. So, for sea otters, brushing their hair is very important.

Identifying Whales

Although there are over fourteen different types of whales that live in Alaska, the gray whale, beluga whale, and orca whale are the most commonly seen within the waters that you will be cruising.

The gray whale is gray in color and typically is covered with scars as well as barnacles. Can you imagine swimming around with barnacles all over your body? Gray whales grow to be very big; the adults can be 36 to 50 feet long and weigh from sixteen to forty-five tons. In comparison a car weighs around a ton, so this means that a gray whale can weigh as much as forty-five cars combined!

The beluga whale is much smaller than the gray whale. Adults grow to be around 11 to 16 feet, and only weigh around 1,000 to

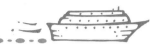

DID YOU KNOW?

Humpback whales travel from Hawaii and California to southeastern Alaska every year. The whales are traveling to and from their original breeding grounds, but there is very little food for them along the way. They don't eat all winter, yet they still have enough energy to travel that far. They can do this because while they are not eating, they are living off the blubber they have stored in their bodies.

DID YOU KNOW?

Salmon is one of the most popular foods in Alaska. The people in Alaska eat salmon like people in most other states eat hamburgers. They make salmon sandwiches, salmon salad, smoked salmon, fried salmon, salmon jerky ... the list goes on. And it's not only the people who eat salmon. Those who live in the deep back country of Alaska feed their sled dogs frozen salmon in the winter.

2,000 pounds. So, a beluga may only weigh about as much as one car. Beluga whales have very smooth skin, just like dolphins, and are very light in color—almost white.

The orca whale—or killer whale—is generally black, with a white belly and other white spots around the body. Orcas have a high fin on their back, which is called a dorsal fin, and this fin can grow to be 6 feet long on some adults. Adult male orcas can grow to be around 23 feet long, so orcas are larger than belugas, but still much smaller than gray whales.

CHAPTER 5

Skagway

GOLD!

Skagway is one town most cruisers especially want to see. The reason? *Gold!* The stampede to Skagway got under-way in the summer of 1897 after two boats from Alaska docked in San Francisco and Seattle. They were carrying the tons of gold the first lucky prospectors had found in the Yukon. It was as if your parents and all their friends dropped everything and rushed to Alaska. Doctors, salesmen, and teachers, people from big cities and small towns—many who had never spent a night in a tent—decided to try for their fortune. Entire families came. More than 100,000 people rushed to Alaska in 1897 and 1898, thinking they would get rich quick.

But fewer than 40,000 of them even reached the gold fields, and most of those people didn't find any gold. A lot of them lost all of their money and possessions. People weren't prepared for how hard the journey would be, especially in winter. They

Web Sites

www.skagway.org is the Web site for Skagway. It will tell you what you can do while you're there.

www.wpyr.com is the Web site for the White Pass and Yukon Route Railroad in Skagway.

www.nps.gov/klgo is the Web site for the Klondike Gold Rush National Historic Park in Skagway.

thought the gold was just on the ground, waiting to be picked up. But instead they had to climb mountains and build boats that could shoot through rapids just to get to the gold fields. Even those who had plenty

of money—some rich people came just for the adventure—couldn't buy food when there wasn't any. One woman, Harriet Pullman, arrived with four kids and seven dollars: She sold pies made from dried apples and baked in dishes she'd pounded from tin cans. The Pullmans ended up richer than a lot of prospectors.

The prospectors changed Alaska and the Yukon forever. Visiting Skagway is a good place to see how. As this was the first stop for many of those heading to the gold fields, it became Alaska's first official city. That's why all fifteen buildings that make up downtown Skagway are part of the National Register of Historic Places. Look at the old buildings and walk the wooden sidewalks, thinking about the town being nearly empty one day and filled with thousands of people a few months later. At one point there were seventy saloons! These days, it's almost the same. In the summer Skagway's population swells from its winter population of fewer than 1,000 people to many times that when two or three cruise ships dock at the same time. How many ships are in Skagway the same day that you are?

Make your first stop the old railroad depot that now is the **National Park Service headquarters,** where you'll find maps for the town and hiking trails and even a little museum about the Gold Rush. Check out all the gear the miners had to carry over the mountains. The rangers here can tell you a lot of interesting things about Skagway history. See if you can find some old pictures of kids who came here with their parents during the Gold Rush.

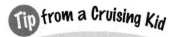

Tip from a Cruising Kid

The train ride in Skagway is really fun, but it takes a long time, so bring something to do.

—EVA, 9, Stamford, Connecticut

Today, lots of backpackers come here to hike the famous **Chilkoot Trail**, which many of the miners took to the gold fields. The trail starts several miles out of town, near what was once a busy town called Dyea. Now there's just a trailhead. The Chilkoot Trail was the shortest and steepest way to the gold fields. "The meanest 33 miles," the miners called it, because they had to climb straight up in places. There were 1,000 snow steps carved straight up the mountainside that the prospectors called "the golden stairs." Look for pictures in town of the miners trying to go up those steps in the snow. Could you do it?

Today the snow steps are gone and the trail is uneven, rocky, muddy, and mostly empty. But during the Gold Rush, it would have been as crowded as a highway at rush hour, with prospectors going in both directions.

Hikers still find shoes and gold pans that were dropped along the way. One fun way to experience the trail is by hiking in a few miles and then taking a float trip along the **Taiya River.** There are many other great hikes around Skagway too. For a short hike lead

your parents to **Lower Dewey Lake**. It's less than a mile, and anyone in town can tell you where to find the trailhead. It's right near the railroad tracks.

Speaking of the railroad tracks . . . be sure to take a ride on the **White Pass and Yukon Route Railway** if you can. This narrow gauge railroad was built over a two-year period in the late 1800s during the frenzy of the Gold Rush. The train was designed to take prospectors from Skagway through the White Pass to the gold fields. Today the railroad operates twice-daily excursions in the summer. The ride is a thrill.

In 1898, hundreds of companies were formed to get people to the gold fields by any means possible—ship, wagon, horse, dogsled, even hot-air balloon! People thought building a railroad through the White Pass was an impossible task, and it nearly was. The railroad climbs 110 miles from sea level up to 2,865 feet. It's one of the steepest railroad grades in North America. The railbed is only 10 feet wide, which is much narrower than that of other trains you've seen. Workers had to haul machinery up

DID YOU KNOW?

Jack London, who wrote the classic books *The Call of the Wild* and *White Fang,* went to the Yukon during the Gold Rush. Poet Robert Service was known for his poems about the Gold Rush. Do you know the story of "The Shooting of Dan McGrew?" If you're lucky, you can listen to Skagway's Buckwheat Donahue tell the tale. Check to see if he's going to be giving a performance at the National Park Service Visitor Center.

DID YOU KNOW?

Skagway has five churches, but just one school for kids from kindergarten through twelfth grade. About 125 kids go to school there.

DID YOU KNOW?

Soapy Smith, Skagway's notorious con man, would collect money from miners to send a telegraph home. But Skagway had no telegraph lines. Smith would also deliver fake telegrams from miners' families asking for money—and then keep the money the miners would give him to send home. He got the name Soapy because he conned miners into buying soap. He later became a town official and a saloon owner. His gang of outlaws helped him to rob and swindle miners until he was gunned down. Find out more about Soapy and his gang at *The Days of 98 Show,* a musical that has been on stage in Skagway for more than seventy years.

DID YOU KNOW?

During the Gold Rush of 1898, 10,000 people lived in Skagway. Today, only about 800 people live here year-round, but each summer more than 750,000 people visit, mostly by ship. Just one big ship docking here can quadruple the town's population—for a few hours anyway!

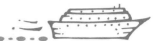

the side of a 1,000-foot cliff. They used 450 tons of explosives to blast the rock out of the way so they could build the track. That's why this small railroad is a prize-winning engineering feat—like the Eiffel Tower, the Panama Canal, or the Statue of Liberty.

Some people like to ride the train far enough to pick up a hiking trail to the Denver or Laughton Glaciers. Most families just take the round-trip ride to the White Pass summit and back again. It's a 20-mile trip that takes a little over three hours. Make sure you bring something to eat. (And sit on the left leaving Skagway for the best view.)

When you ride the old train—some of the cars are more than one hundred years old—think about the railroad workers and the prospectors who made their way up the White Pass by foot and on horseback before the railroad was built. Watch for Gold Rush Cemetery, where the swindler Soapy Smith is buried. You should be able to see the Harding Glacier when you get to Rocky Point. The conductors will tell you what you're passing and you can follow the route on a map they'll give you when you board. Did you see Pitchfork Falls? Look for other falls along the way. How many did you see? When the train whistles, get ready! You're going to plunge into Tunnel Mountain, carved 1,000 feet above the gulch. After you get out of the tunnel, watch for Bridal Veil Falls and Dead Horse Gulch, named for the 3,000 pack animals that died here because they were overloaded and neglected or abandoned during the year of 1898.

Congratulations! You made it to the White Pass Summit. Could you have done it carrying a ton of gear?

And for the prospectors, getting here wasn't the only hard part. The gold wasn't just lying on the ground waiting for them. You'll see how hard it is once you try gold panning.

Remember, it's all in the wrist!

Going Ashore

Most days of your cruise, the ship will stop at different towns so that you and your family can get off the boat, sightsee, shop, and have fun hiking, rafting, kayaking, fishing, or walking on a glacier. Many families like to plan what they're going to do on shore before they leave for Alaska and then arrange the activities with the cruise line. Write down the towns where your ship stopped . . . and what you did while you were there.

1. _____

2. _____

3. _____

4. _____

5. _____

6. _____

7. _____

8. _____

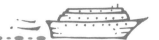

Shopping List

Prospectors had to lug a ton of supplies up to the top of the
Chilkoot and White Passes in the snow before Canada's Mounties
would allow them into Canada and onto the gold fields. The
Mounties wanted to make sure that everyone had enough food
and clothes to survive—there were no stores. It took the prospectors
as many as thirty backbreaking trips to get their gear to the top of
the pass. Here's just some of what they were required to bring:

- 350 pounds of flour
- 150 pounds of bacon
- 100 pounds of beans
- 100 pounds of sugar
- 1 tin of matches
- 2 axes
- 20 pounds of nails
- Frying pan
- 3 suits of long underwear
- 6 pairs of heavy wool socks
- 2 pairs of rubber boots

Panning for Gold

"It's all in the wrist." At least that's the advice from Buckwheat Donahue, Skagway's four-time gold-panning champion. Head to a stream or river and take your gold miner's tin pan. Fill it with gravel from the edge of the river, adding water until the pan is just about full, and then shake the pan from side to side. The heavier gold flakes will settle at the bottom so when you dip the pan in and out of the water the top layer of dirt and pebbles will wash away. All that's left should be the gold! It's hard work. You can pan for gold at any stream or at Liarsville, a reconstructed miners camp in Skagway. Try Liarsville Gold Rush Trail Camp of 1898 (call 907–983–3000 for info.) Or Klondike Gold Dredge Tours (www.klondikegolddredge.com; phone 907–983–3197).

Eagles

Eagles mate for life and like many families, live in the same homes (called aeries) for years. Their nests, high in the trees, can weigh hundreds of pounds, and measure six feet or more across. Like kids, baby eaglets are watched constantly by their parents! But they can fly a lot sooner than babies can walk—way before they're a year old. Look for eagles to swoop down and grab fish for dinner. You may see eagles near Skagway or at the Bald Eagle Preserve near Haines, where thousands of eagles gather—more than anywhere else in the world. Take a float trip through the preserve to see them. Keep your camera handy.

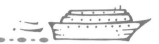

DID YOU KNOW?

Prospectors were called Sourdoughs because they carried sourdough starter—a mixture of yeast, flour, and water—in bags around their necks to make bread and pancakes. All they'd need to do was add water and mix up their meal. If they remembered to add water and flour after each use, the starter would last a long time.

When you get home, here's how you can make your own starter: Mix three cups of flour and three cups of warm water plus one tablespoon of sugar and one packet (or one tablespoon) of dry yeast in a glass or ceramic bowl. Do not use metal or plastic. Cover with a cloth and let it stand at room temperature for two days. Your mixture should be bubbly and smell sour. After two days in a warm place, store covered in the fridge. You can use as much as you need at a time, letting it stand in the kitchen until it gets bubbly again.

Here's a recipe for sourdough pancakes from Kirsten Dixon, who is a well-known Alaskan chef.

- 3/4 cup sourdough starter
- 1 egg, slightly beaten
- 1 cup water
- 2 teaspoons safflower oil
- 1/3 cup dry powdered milk
- 1 cup flour
- 1 teaspoon baking soda
- 1 1/2 tablespoons sugar

Combine the sourdough starter, egg, water, and oil. In another bowl combine powdered milk, flour, baking soda, and sugar. Stir to blend. Add the dry ingredients to the sourdough and mix until smooth. Pour batter in pancake portions onto a greased nonstick griddle. When the pancake tops get bubbly, turn them over and cook briefly on the other side. Dig in!

Skagway Scavenger Hunt

As you and your family walk around town, see how many of these you can find.

___ Ship captains' signatures on a cliff wall

___ A gold nugget

___ A picture of a kid from the 1890s (*Hint:* Try the National Historical Park Visitor Center in the old railroad depot.)

___ Soapy Smith's grave

___ Dead Horse Gulch

___ A photo of the 1898 miners on the "Golden Stairs" (*Hint:* Look in the visitor center again.)

___ A backpacker

___ An old-fashioned train

___ The old White Pass and Yukon Railroad depot

___ A helicopter

___ A bald eagle

___ Someone wearing a Skagway T-shirt

___ Alaska's oldest hotel (think Golden . . .)

CHAPTER 6

Juneau

Welcome to the city of the big Gs. Stumped? Juneau is famous for its Glaciers, for Gold, and of course for Government. It's the capital of Alaska. You can see the Capitol building and where the governor of Alaska lives. In fact Juneau was one of the first towns in Alaska founded after the United States bought Alaska from Russia. Now, it's the biggest city in this part of the state—especially in summer when all of the cruise ship passengers, like you, come to visit. Nearly three-quarters of a million people visit each year. No wonder the streets are so busy.

Alaska's number one tourist attraction is just outside Juneau: the **Mendenhall Glacier,** towering 800 feet above the surface of the lake. What's even more amazing is this huge ice cube is only one part of the Juneau Icefield. In some places the ice is more than a mile thick and, deep down, hundreds of years old. If you go out to see the Mendenhall, try one of the telescopes at the visitor center to get a closer view of the glacier ice. The Forest Service guides can tell you everything you want to know about the glacier or lead you on a hike nearby. There are many short trails that start right at the visitor center. There are helicopter trips that will take you right onto the icefield so that you can hike around on a glacier or go dogsledding. Some people have even gotten married on this

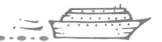

glacier! But you can have fun in Juneau without taking a helicopter—or getting married. You can hike, kayak, mountain bike, canoe, pan for gold—even check out a rain forest.

That's right, there's a temperate rain forest here. Temperate means it's cooler than a tropical rain forest, but just as wet. From Franklin Street right near the cruise ship dock you can ride the **Mount Roberts Tram** more than 1,800 feet up through the rain forest, get out, and hike down. There's a cool nature center at the top too, where you might see some native Alaskans carving wood or ivory. Keep an eye out for totem pole carvings along the trail as well. And don't forget to bring some snacks for the hike back! It's about a mile and a half back to the tram base. If you're not up for the hike, you can also look around at the top and ride the tram down.

Many people go whale watching or fishing in Juneau. If you head out on a whale-watching boat, you're sure to see humpback whales. If you go fishing, no one can promise you'll catch a fish,

DID YOU KNOW?

The word *musher* comes from the French word *marcher,* which means "to walk." During the Gold Rush, anyone who was traveling to the gold fields was called a "marcher," which got changed to "musher." The name stuck to people who run dogs outdoors.

DID YOU KNOW?

You can rent a fishing pole and catch some salmon right in the waters off Juneau. Grab a taxi to the **Macaulay Salmon Hatchery,** which has a sport fishing dock. You'll see thousands of salmon returning from the ocean back to where they were raised. You'll also see seals and other animals feeding on the fish. Inside is a big aquarium.

DID YOU KNOW?

Admiralty Island, near Juneau, has more brown bears than anywhere else in the world.

DID YOU KNOW?

The winter climate in Juneau is similar to the temperature in Seattle. Local kids like to ski, snowboard, and go sledding in the mountains, where it's a little colder and there's plenty of snow.

DID YOU KNOW?

You can only get to Juneau by boat, ferry, or plane, because it's surrounded by mountains, glaciers, and water. The city is named after Joe Juneau, a gold prospector who struck it rich in the 1880s. But the first people to live here were the Tlingit, thousands of years before Joe and the other prospectors got here. A lot of people say a Tlingit chief told Joe where to look for the gold. You can take a tour of an old mine here at the **Alaska-Gastineau Mill and Gold Mine Tour** (P.O. Box 34105, Juneau, AK 99803; 907–463–3900).

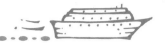

but there are lots of salmon and halibut in the water. Some halibut weigh more than one hundred pounds. Keep an eye out for bald eagles in the trees near the shore. While you're looking for them, they're looking for food. You won't have trouble finding food for yourself in Juneau—especially salmon.

Make sure to leave some time for Juneau's museums too. The **Alaska State Museum** (395 Whittier Street; 907–465–2901) is a great place to find out all about Alaska—from the native cultures to the Gold Rush. There's a great kids area too and special *Kids Gazette* magazines to make your museum going more fun. Don't miss the 34-foot-long boat called a *umiak* that's in the Eskimo gallery, or the amazing clan house in the

Northwest Coast Indians area. Climb to the second floor of the museum, up a ramp that surrounds a big tree, and you'll see an eagle nest in its branches. If you like hunting for treasures, you'll like the Gold Rush area of the museum—especially since you'll be visiting Skagway, where prospectors started their trek over the mountains to the gold fields. You'll see all kinds of things the prospectors used, from the kind of scale they needed to weigh their gold nuggets to the first-aid kit they had to carry along in case they got hurt. The kids area has interesting things to do. There's a big ship model of the *Discovery,* the ship Captain George Vancouver used when he explored Alaska. You can dress up and board the ship.

Alaska Marine Highway

There aren't always roads to take you where you want to go in Alaska. That's why people often use small planes. Maybe you've flown in one already. Many other people travel by ferry on Alaska's Marine Highway. The ferries travel year-round, all along the Pacific Coast from Bellingham, Washington, through British Columbia—3,500 miles! People bring their cars or RVs on the ferries. You'll probably

see them in the towns you visit during your cruise. Alaskans hop the ferries all the time.

Talk to the Dogs

Danny Seavey was eighteen when he competed in the Iditarod dogsled race, the famous race from Juneau to Nome that takes place every March. His father and grandfather also were racing that year. It was the first time three generations of the same family were in the race. You might get to go dogsledding near Juneau or Skagway. Here are some of the commands Danny Seavey and other racers use for their dogs: Think any of them would work with your dog— or little brother?

Gee: Go to the right.

Haw: Go to the left.

Whoa: Stop.

Hike: Go straight ahead.

An Alaskan Kid Says

It's never too cold to play outside. There's always something fun to do, so you just do it. Like skiing, or snowball fights, or sledding. When we get cold, we just go in and warm up. Sometimes we have hot chocolate. We also play computer games and board games if we are playing inside.

—SPENCER, 12, Girdwood

Souvenir Smarts

Juneau is a great place to souvenir shop, whether you'd like a cuddly bear or moose, a totem pole, a sweatshirt with a big fish on it, a lollipop shaped like an animal (try the Alaskan Fudge Company on Franklin Street), Alaska posters and stickers, or gold nuggets. It's a good idea to talk to your mom and dad about what you want to buy and how much you can spend before hitting the stores. Some kids like to buy one big souvenir. Others would rather start a collection. You could get pins from every place you've stopped on the cruise, decals (they're great to decorate water bottles and lunch boxes), or even postcards. Write something on the back of the postcard so you remember what you did the day you got it. Then mail it to yourself at home!

CHAPTER 7

The First Alaskans

Respect your elders! Sure, that's what you've always been taught. But do you always follow that advice? Among Alaska's native peoples, however, the elders *are* the ones who are considered the smartest and wisest, always.

Before the Europeans came to Alaska, the native tribes didn't mix much with each other and spoke different languages. Kids in those different tribes were as different as you might be from kids growing up in another country, speaking another language. Many scientists believe that the first people arrived in Alaska thousands of years ago, probably from Siberia. If you look on a map, you'll see that Russia is pretty close to Alaska. You might meet some native peoples on your trip. Ask them about their tribes.

Web Site

www.alaskanative.net is the Web site for the Alaska Native Heritage Center.

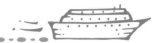

The Tlingit (pronounced *Klink'-it*) live in Southeast Alaska. Tradition-ally, they built big houses near good fishing and traveled by kayaks and canoes. They built their canoes and houses from the giant cedar trees growing along the coast. The entrances to their houses always faced the sea.

The Haida and the Mximshian are smaller tribes related to the Tlingit. You might meet some members in Sitka or Juneau. They continue to be known for their beautiful weaving and, of course, their totem poles.

Today, members of the Athabascan tribe live around Fairbanks, as well as in more remote places in the Alaskan interior, rather than along the coast. They traditionally hunted caribou. Everyone in the family helped with the hunt—even the kids. The families would follow the caribou, moose, and other animals from place to place, rather than living in one town. Their clothing was made of caribou hide.

Inuit Eskimos live in northern Alaska near the Bering Sea. They think it's warm when the temperature rises to about freezing! In the old days they hunted for whales in spring, fished in summer, prepared their houses for winter in fall, and seal-hunted under the ice in winter. Men would camp on the ice and watch for whales.

???

DID YOU KNOW?

Eskimo ice cream is called *akutaq* and is made with whipped berries, seal oil, and freshly fallen snow.

DID YOU KNOW?

Alaska's native peoples make up roughly 15 percent of the state's population. Most are Eskimo, American Indian, and Aleut, but Alaska natives rarely refer to each other this way. They describe themselves based on their tribe and where they're from, such as "I'm Yup'ik from Bethel." Alaska natives are those who are from one of the five major native groups. A good book about Alaska's native kids is *Children of the Midnight Sun*, by Tricia Brown.

DID YOU KNOW?

No one in Alaska ever really lived in igloos. Houses were built of sod or wood. Igloos were only made for temporary shelters along the trails or while camping and fishing on ice.

That's when they built and used igloos. They still depend on whales and seals. If you go to a museum in Juneau or Anchorage, you might see Inuit Eskimo masks that represent animal spirits.

Aleuts still live on the Aleutian Islands on the southwest coast of Alaska and were among the first Alaska natives to have contact and conflicts with Europeans who, like the pioneers in the Lower 48, helped themselves to whatever they wanted. In those days the Aleuts lived in communal sod-covered dwellings looking out

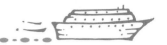

toward the sea. Their houses, called *barbaras*, were underground to protect them from the winds, but the houses included skylights to let the sun and air in and to let smoke from cooking fires out. The Aleuts relied on salmon and other sea life for food. They made baskets from grass so strong that they could use the baskets to carry water.

You might get to meet some native kids in one of the towns that you visit. Talk to them. You'll learn that their lives are a mix of cultures—and circumstances. For example, instead of taking a bus to play another school in a sport, they take a plane. Instead of having one dog, they might have a team of sled dogs. Are their lives much different than yours? You probably all watch the same TV shows!

Mukluks and Muktuk

Don't get these two mixed up! *Mukluks* are lightweight boots that are traditionally made with seal skin soles and fur. *Muktuk* is an Eskimo treat made out of skin and whale blubber. Eskimos eat it fresh, frozen, or boiled.

Native Words

There were once twenty different native languages in Alaska, but now only a handful are in use. Most Alaska natives speak English. Here are some examples of native languages:

- Eagle would be *tsaak* in Haida, *chak* in Tlingit, and *lack-sh-geeg* in Tsimshian.
- Kayak is *iqyax* in Aleut.
- *Inuit* is the Eskimo name for themselves, meaning "the people."

Ask the Alaska natives you meet how to say your name in their language. Then ask them to teach you how to say "Thank you."

Regalia

The traditional outfits worn by the Tlingit, Haida, and Tsimshian people on special occasions show which clan they belong to. These special clothes include robes, tunics, beaded headbands, moccasins, and special hats made out of cedar bark or spruce root. Their robes were woven by women, based on designs men had created. The women used yellow, blue-green, and black dyes. If you see a native performance, the dancers likely will be wearing their native costumes.

Draw a picture of the "regalia" you'd design for yourself.

CHAPTER 8

Smaller Stops Along the Way

Bigger doesn't always mean better. Some of Alaska's smaller towns, like Ketchikan, Sitka, Wrangell, or Petersburg, are a lot of fun. During your cruise, you won't be able to see all of them. But we think you'll find something interesting to do at every stop.

In **Ketchikan** check out those totem poles! That's what everybody wants to see when they first get to Ketchikan. People believe that the name *Ketchikan* came from a Tlingit word that means "where the eagles' wings are." But it ought to mean where the totem poles are. There are more totems at the **Totem Heritage Center** in Ketchikan than anywhere else in the United States.

These poles were brought here from uninhabited Tlingit and Haida village sites near Ketchikan native villages, where they had

Web Sites

www.nps.gov/webrangers is a National Park Service Web site for kids.

www.visit-Ketchikan.com is the Web site for the town of Ketchikan and can tell you about things to do there.

www.Sitka.com will tell you what there is to do when you get to Sitka.

www.Wrangell.com is the site for finding fun and games in Wrangell.

www.Alaskaraptor.org will fill you in on bald eagles and the amazing Alaska Raptor Center.

been carved from cedar logs more than one hundred years ago. Craftspeople still make totem poles today. You might see carvers at work with special tools that they make themselves. Other native artists might be weaving baskets or working with beads.

Just across a footbridge from the heritage center is the **Deer Mountain Tribal Hatchery.** You might be able to see a bald eagle there, and you'll certainly see lots of salmon. They're sent into local waters from here when they're big enough. Ask anyone in Ketchikan and they'll tell you they've got the best salmon fishing in all of south-eastern Alaska. Got a fishing rod handy?

If you like totem poles, you can see even more of them a few miles outside of town at **Saxman Native Village Totem Pole Park.** There, you are likely to see carvers at work and old poles that were brought here in the 1930s, as well as ones that have been carved since. You can't miss the Sun and Raven pole at the entrance to the park. There are even more poles about 10 miles from Ketchikan at Totem Bright State Historical Park, where there's also a community house called a clan house that could have housed as many as fifty people.

Of course there's much more to do in Ketchikan than look at totem poles. Kids always enjoy the **Great Alaskan Lumberjack Show,** where guys compete to see who can climb up a tall tree, chop one down, or make logs roll with their feet. Have you ever seen a log-rolling contest? It's a lot of fun.

There are plenty of places to get souvenirs too, especially from the different tribes. That's because the Ketchikan area is home to the Tlingit, Haida, and Tsimshian Nations.

Some people like to take a floatplane or a boat to a place called **Misty Fjords** to see the giant cliffs and maybe a whale or a bear fishing for salmon along the shore. This is a great place to kayak too.

Sitka is another small town in southeastern Alaska. It was actually the capital of the state from 1895 until 1906. Before that, it was the place where a lot of Russians lived when they traded furs here. There's still a big Russian church in Sitka, St. Michael's Cathedral, right in the town center. The Tlingit people were here first and fought the Russians, because they resented their arrival. Eventually, the Tlingit were forced to move, and they rebuilt their homes around the Russian encampment. When the fur trade declined, Russia sold Alaska to the United

States. Today, you can see a real mix of cultures in the buildings and the shops. You might be able to see a Tlingit dance performance. Like a lot of towns and cities in Alaska, you can only get here by plane or boat.

This isolation doesn't bother the wildlife, of course. And you should see plenty around here, especially at the **Alaska Raptor Center,** where you can get close to bald eagles and other Alaskan birds. Sitka even has a **Whale Park** where from shore you might be able to see humpbacks, sea lions, sea otters, and more. There are plenty of places to go bike riding or hiking too. You can walk to the **Indian River Trail** from downtown. It will take you through the rain forest!

If you get to **Wrangell,** don't miss **Petroglyph Beach,** about a mile out of town on Evergreen Avenue. Petroglyphs are carvings on rocks and here they're found on boulders. There are about forty images in all—faces, fish, and seashells. You can also see an old tribal clan house on Chief Shakes Island here. The island is in the middle of Wrangell Harbor. But you can get to it on a walkway.

DID YOU KNOW?

Raptors are birds of prey—meat eaters that hunt for food. They've all got good eyesight, strong feet with sharp talons, and a hooked sharp beak. Can you name some raptors? (*Hint:* Some go "hoot" in the night.)

DID YOU KNOW?

"Sitka Slippers" are what Alaskans call the really heavy rubber boots they wear in the rain.

DID YOU KNOW?

The Trans-Alaska Pipeline carries about 1.8 million barrels of oil every day from the North Slope to the port of Valdez. That's enough to "fill up" a lot of cars and heat a lot of homes.

DID YOU KNOW?

More Native Americans live in Ketchikan than anywhere else in Alaska.

DID YOU KNOW?

At least a third of all the people who visit Alaska come by cruise ship. The top ten states sending visitors to Alaska are California, Washington, Florida, Texas, New York, Oregon, Illinois, Michigan, and Colorado. Are you from one of these states?

DID YOU KNOW?

Bald eagles have more than 7,000 feathers.

DID YOU KNOW?

The United States purchased Alaska for $7.2 million—about two cents an acre. What a deal!

Your ship might stop at **Petersburg**—a place called "Little Norway" because it was founded by a Norwegian named Peter Buschmann, who came here with others to fish. Some of the families have lived in Petersburg for five generations! Has your family

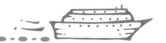

been in the same town that long?

One of the most fun things to do in Petersburg—and in the other towns—is to watch the fishing boats.

How many different kinds of fish do you see? How many have you tasted in Alaska?

Sound Like an Alaskan

Outside is anywhere that's not in the Yukon or Alaska.

Spring break-up is when the ice on rivers breaks up and washes away. Some people also call it spring break-up when couples who spent the cold winter together break up!

Sourdough is what an old-timer in Alaska is called.

Cheechako is Alaskan for a newcomer.

Skookum means strong and useful.

Termination dust is the first snow of the season. In the old days that was a sign to prospectors to start wrapping up or terminating their season's work.

Totem Poles

Totem poles tell the story of a person or a family. Often they are finished for a big celebration, like a wedding. Or for a big event, like building a new house. Or to honor someone who has died. Usually the carvers pick big cedar trees. They cut them down and then split the tree in two. The part chosen for the pole is hollowed out from the middle. You will see a lot of the same symbols on different poles, but they won't look exactly the same. You'll see a lot of poles at the **Totem Heritage Center** in Ketchikan. See if you can find:

___ a raven   ___ a frog

___ an eagle   ___ a killer whale

___ a bear   ___ a wolf

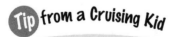 **Tip** from a Cruising Kid

Going on a floatplane was so fun.

–EMILIE, 10, Detroit, Michigan

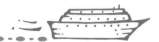

What symbols would you use on a totem pole to tell the story of your family? Use this space to draw a totem pole.

More About the Eagle Hospital

It started with one injured bald eagle more than thirty years ago. Today, the **Alaska Raptor Center** in Sitka treats 200 injured birds each year. Some birds have collided with power lines or cars, swallowed poisonous chemicals, or gotten tangled in fishing lines. The center hopes to help them heal and then release them back into the wild. In some cases the birds wouldn't survive if they were left to fend for themselves, so they go to a zoo or live at the center's seventeen-acre campus, where you can visit them. Take a two-hour trek through the bald eagle hospital and learn about owls and other raptors as well as eagles. For each area at the center you visit, you get a stamp in your "passport" and learn how you can make a difference for wild animals.

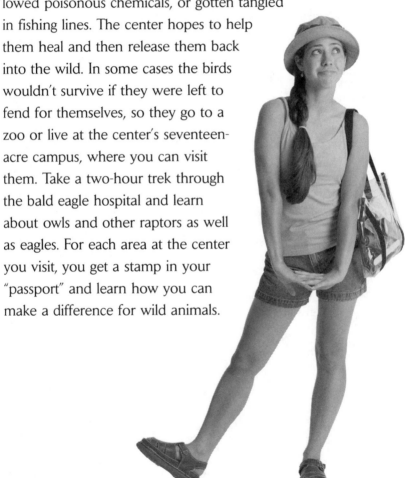

CHAPTER 9

Denali National Park

Got your camera? Denali National Park is a stop that many families make either before or after their cruise. Denali is one of the best places in the world to view amazing wildlife in its natural environ-ment. Because the park is just 300 miles south of the Arctic Circle, there are twenty-plus hours of daylight in the summertime. This makes it seem like you can never run out of time to do all the things you want to do—until you get too tired! You can go hik-ing, biking, fishing, rafting, and hunt for gold. You can even go horseback riding; there are trails right outside of the park because the park's trails aren't made to support horse traffic. Just don't for-get to pack some bug spray and sunscreen.

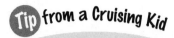

Tip from a Cruising Kid

Go horseback riding right outside of Denali National Park. It's really fun to go up the steep trails.

—EVA, 9, Stamford, Connecticut

Not only is Denali National Park huge, spread over six million acres, but it is also home of Mount McKinley. At 20,320 feet high, it is the tallest mountain in all of North America. A lot of people like to take a flight-seeing tour of the mountain. Mount McKinley could be the most unique mountain in the world. Other, higher peaks—such as Everest, K2, and Aconcagua (in Argentina), which rise from 2,000 to 10,000 feet higher than McKinley—are all part of enormous mountain ranges. But McKin-ley rises all alone. Of course McKinley is part of a mountain range—the Alaska Range—which holds some impressive peaks. But McKinley is so much bigger than its surroundings it makes the range's other large mountains look like foothills.

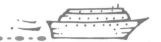

Mount McKinley is so big that it even creates its own weather. It could be a beautiful day down in Denali National Park, while storms are battering the slopes of McKinley, with the weather at minus thirty degrees with winds at 100 miles per hour. The best time to catch a glimpse of the mountain is early on a summer morning. The mountain can actually be hard to see in the summertime, because some of it is often hidden by clouds. Even if you can't see the peak, though, you'll still be able to see some of the mountain. And even if it rains during your visit, you can still get out and have fun. Just don't forget your rain jacket and hiking boots.

Go for a hike with your family on one of the trails. How many different color wildflowers do you see . . . pink . . . purple . . . yellow . . . red? You'll probably be able to pick some wild blue-

Web Site

www.denalinationalpark.com
is the Web site for the park.

berries and eat them right along the trail. Make believe you're an animal looking for food. What would you be? Bear . . . eagle . . . moose?

Most of the land in the park is tundra, which here means it's above the tree line. Be sure to check out a Denali Discovery Pack from the visitor center. It'll add to your fun along the way. You can become a Junior Ranger. Just ask the park rangers what you need to do. The rangers lead a lot of hikes and other activities for families too. There are lodges and hotels near the park, with plenty of bikes, fishing gear, and more. At some places they even tell Alaskan stories at night and have sled dogs. You can meet some sled dogs at the Kantishna Roadhouse, a backcountry lodge deep in the park.

Don't miss the chance to pan for gold. Your hotel can set you up with someone who can teach you how to do it. Don't worry about bringing your own pan, they will have plenty that you can use. You can pretend to be an old rusher during the Alaska Gold Rush and learn to do it the way those prospectors really did, dipping their pans in the icy water. You might even find pieces of gold in the Denali rivers!

Whatever you do, you want to watch for animals. You should see plenty because there are thousands of animals that make this park their home.

Chances are you might see moose first because they often gather pretty close to the park headquarters. They eat up to sixty

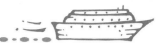

pounds of leaves a day! This is also one of the few places in the world to see grizzly bears in the wild. Black bears are harder to spot. You also will see birds of all kinds in the park. Willow ptarmigan—Alaska's state bird—live here year-round, changing colors with the seasons to blend in with their surroundings.

But take the rangers' advice and don't get too close to the animals at Denali. Remember—the park is their home; you're the visitor here.

Working on the Railroad

How would you like to ride a train all summer talking about yourself? That's what some Alaska high school kids do on the Alaska Railroad. You'll see them on the train to Denali (or Seward) walking around with their scrapbooks, telling passengers of what it's like to grow up in Alaska. It's not an easy job to get. They have to take a ten-week class to make sure they can answer all sorts of questions about Alaska. What question wouls you ask first?

Denali's Back Door

You'll probably pass **Talkeetna** on the way to Denali. It's a tiny town that's called "the back door to Denali." Only about 800 people live here—how many live in your hometown? Can you imagine living in a town that small? Talkeetna is where all the mountaineers who plan to climb the famous Mount McKinley gear up for their climb. What would you ask a climber if you met one?

???

DID YOU KNOW?
Denali is a tribal Athabascan word that means "the high one," and was the original name of Mount McKinley. The Athabascans who named Denali believed the mountain was the home of the sun. The original name of the park was Mount McKinley National Park, and in 1896 the mountain's name was switched to McKinley for William McKinley, the twenty-fifth president of the United States. But in 1975 the state officially returned the park to the native, and much more fitting name of Denali. The official name of the mountain, however, remains Mount McKinley.

DID YOU KNOW?
Denali National Park covers more than six million acres. This is larger than the state of Massachusetts.

Climbing Mount McKinley

Because Mount McKinley is the highest peak in North America, reaching its summit has been a dream for most mountaineers since the first expedition made it to the top of South Peak—the highest peak on the mountain—more than ninety years ago. Even kids have made it. About a dozen people under eighteen years old climb the mountain each year. A few of these people are around twelve, but the majority are fifteen and older. The youngest person to ever summit the mountain is Galen Johnston, who was eleven years old when he reached the top in 2001. About 1,000 climbers

attempt to summit the mountain every year, but usually only about half succeed—the other half have to turn around because of bad weather, or bad luck. Could you make it?

On the Road

Only one road leads into Denali National Park. After the first stretch, cars are limited to those that have special permits. That's why many people who visit Denali take a long shuttle bus ride on a park service bus through the park. The trip takes all day, so bring along some snacks. You'll also be able to get off the bus and hike around. Watch for Denali's animals through the window. Which ones did you see?

___ grizzly bears   ___ wolves   ___ Dall sheep

___ caribou   ___ moose   ___ foxes

___ beavers

Hiking Smarts

One of the best ways to have fun in the park is to go hiking. There are many routes that you and your family could take around the park, including hiking trails and cross-country routes. Here's what you need to make your trek enjoyable:

• Pick a hike that will be fun for you to go on, and not too hard. A park ranger or lodge worker will be able to tell you the difficulty levels of the routes, so choose one that you will like.

- Remember to be ready for the park's changing weather. The weather can go from hot and sunny to cold and drizzly within an hour, so it is important to dress accordingly. You should wear layers. That way, if you get too hot, you can take something off. Also, when it comes to hikes, cotton clothing is not your friend. Once cotton gets wet, it does not dry and can make you very cold. Being cold and wet on a hike is no fun.

- Don't forget your rain gear!

- Bring plenty of snacks (some trail mix or M&Ms) as hiking can definitely work up an appetite. Remember to bring along plenty of water as well.

- Don't forget your binoculars and camera. You will probably see a lot of really cool animals that you won't find anywhere else, and you will have many great picture opportunities.

- Keep in mind that this park is not a zoo. Although the animals may seem accustomed to people, you have to remember that they are still wild. So, keep your distance and be safe!

An Alaskan Kid Says

When it's too cold too play outside, we do normal kid stuff. Play games, do homework, use the Internet, see movies, go shopping.

–ELIZABETH, 16, Anchorage

CHAPTER 10

Vancouver and Seattle

Some Alaskan cruises these days either start or end in Vancouver, British Columbia, in Canada, or Seattle, Washington. That means you'll get to see more than Alaska on your trip, and maybe even experience the culture of another country—Canada.

Vancouver

Welcome to one of the coolest cities anywhere. You can shop till you drop (kids say CDs can be bargains here). Eat till you're stuffed, in-line skate, swim, meet a beluga whale, wander around the Chinatown Night Market, or visit unusual museums.

A lot of the best stuff in Vancouver happens in **Stanley Park,** right in the middle of the city. The park is one of the places kids love most here. You'll see kids along the park's seawall, riding bikes, skateboarding, and looking at the giant totem poles. You can rent a bike or Roller Blades and ride all along the seawall too. It goes for miles. Just make sure to stay on the correct side of the path—one side is for people who are walking or jogging. Watch for signs and the way everyone else is going. Check out the "9 o'clock Gun" at the water's edge. In the old days it was fired to help ships set their clocks. Today, it's fired every night at 9:00 P.M. Did you hear the cannon's rumble?

While you're in the park, you might see people playing

A Vancouver Kid Says

It's really fun to go to the seawall and waterslides in Stanley Park.

–SCOTT, 8

www.seeseattle.org is a good place to check out what's happening in Seattle.

www.seattleaquarium.org is the Seattle Aquarium's Web site and also will tell you a lot about sea life in the Pacific Northwest.

www.pikeplacemarket.org/about/kidsstuff/ is the area of Seattle's Pike Place Market that's especially for kids.

www.tourismvancouver.com is the Web site for Vancouver and will help you plan your visit.

www.vanaqua.org is the Web site for the Vancouver Aquarium, with lots about whales.

www.granvilleisland.bc.ca is the Web site for Granville Island in Vancouver, which is a shopping and entertainment mecca for kids as well as adults.

a game that doesn't look familiar—it's called cricket. Kids and grown-ups play cricket in Canada the way folks in the United States play baseball. Cricket is a game played on a team with bats and balls but with different rules. Which sport do you think looks like more fun?

Stanley Park is home to all kinds of birds, ducks, geese, and swans. You might see baby ducklings trailing behind their mom. See how many different birds you can find.

Whales live in Stanley Park too—at the **Vancouver Aquarium.** It's famous for the research that scientists here do on whales. You can watch the orcas at feeding time or get up close to a giant white beluga. Canada has more belugas than any other kind of whale. Some people think belugas should only be in the wild, but scientists at the aquarium say having them there allows people to see them and helps the scientists who study them. The aquarium also lets you get an up-close look at other sea life that lives in the Pacific Northwest: sea otters, dolphins, even a giant octopus! You'll see whales on the giant totem poles near Brockton Point, in Stanley Park. The bears represent power on the land; the killer whales rule the sea.

Of course Stanley Park isn't the only place that's fun in Vancouver. You'll notice that Vancouver has a lot of waterfront, where you can take sailing or windsurfing lessons or go to the beach—there are ten beaches right in the city. Pick up a free copy of "Kids Guide to Vancouver" at the visitor information center at the airport or the visitor center in the city.

There are also many good places to eat in Vancouver. Have a ginger tea at a Chinese tea shop, popcorn in the park, Chinese stir fry, freshly caught fish, or burgers and fries, naturally. For a real adventure head out to the **Capilano Suspension Bridge and Park** about ten minutes from downtown in North Vancouver. Here's your chance to run across a swaying bridge—230 feet above the Capilano River. At 450 feet long and so high off the ground, it's better than a lot of theme park rides!

Once you're out at the Suspension Bridge and Park, you'll see that there's a **Totem Park** with more than poles. Stop in the Big House carving center, where you can see native carvers at work. Ask questions. They'll be glad to tell you how they learned to carve a pole.

In Vancouver, you can learn more about West Coast native cultures at the **Vancouver Museum** and at the **University of British Columbia's Museum of Anthropology.** Kids especially like the Haida House complex just outside the museum, which includes a large native house and several totem poles.

Leave time for shopping. **Granville Island**—connected to downtown by the Granville Bridge right near Anderson Street—has a **Kids Market** with twenty-five different shops chock full of stuff kids like, including toys, stuffed animals, magic tricks, even treats for your dogs. Bring your bathing suit because there's a big free water park outside. And if you get hungry, there's the huge Public Market, where you can watch bagels being baked, toffee being made, and donuts being fried while musicians and magicians entertain the crowds outdoors. You can hop a ferry or walk over the bridge to the island.

Gastown is the oldest part of Vancouver (at Hastings Street and Water Street) and a good place to souvenir hunt and eat too. It got its name from a guy who lived here who was nicknamed Gassy Jack Deighton. Check out the two-ton Gastown Steam

Clock (it's on the corner of Cambie Street). It sends out clouds of steam every hour. Hungry? You're right near Chinatown (around Main Street and Keefer). There are barrels of live eels, streetlights decorated with dragons, strange-smelling herbs, and Chinese chefs cooking everywhere. Egg roll, anyone?

Seattle

One of the places in Seattle that is the most fun is the giant **Pike Place Market.** It's the first stop for many kids, who rush to see **Rachel,** the giant piggy bank in front of the market. You can crawl on her or give her money; the pig collects thousands of dollars each year to help needy kids and grown-ups in Seattle.

There's so much food at Pike Place you'll have trouble figuring out what to eat: a Washington apple or home-baked cookie, honey stick or Russian pastry. The market was established nearly one hundred years ago so farmers could bring their produce to the city and sell it directly to the people who lived there. You can meet farmers from all over Washington State at Pike Place. Some of their families have been selling here since the market opened! Did you know that Washington grows more apples than any other state? You'll see lots of people selling fish here too. Washington fishermen catch more than two billion pounds ever year: salmon, halibut, mussels, and shrimp. What's your favorite kind of seafood?

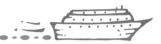

Here's your chance to try food you've never had—spicy jelly flavored hazelnuts, yellow cherries, or green eggs. You'll find those at **Pike Place Creamery** in the Sanitary Market Building. (Moo as you go by; it's a Seattle tradition!) Other tasty stops are the **Donut Robot** in the Economy Building and **Starbucks,** on Pike Place, the only street through the market. This market is where Starbucks coffee started. Of course you can buy souvenirs here, everything from old comic books to necklaces and funny T-shirts. What did you buy?

It's hard to believe the buildings that hold this bustling market were almost torn down. Luckily, the people of Seattle voted to preserve it, and now this market is a national historic district. More than nine million people visit here each year.

Take a short walk to the **Seattle Art Museum.** Make sure to see the huge sculpture, *Hammering Man,* outside. There are day-long family programs and a Please-Touch room for kids on the third floor.

You can head to the waterfront from the market too—just go down all the stairs known as the "Hillclimb." There's a waterfront trolley that will take you everyplace you want to go, like **Pioneer Square,** the oldest part of Seattle, where prospectors left to board ships for gold country during the big Klondike Gold Rush. You can buy your own gold nugget here at a store in the Pioneer Square neighborhood.

Don't miss the **Seattle Aquarium.** This is the place to find out all you want to know about salmon and the other creatures living

DID YOU KNOW?

The Sam Kee Building in Vancouver's Chinatown is one of the skinniest in the world—just six feet wide. Vancouver has the third-largest Chinatown in North America. After English, Chinese is the most common language spoken in Vancouver.

DID YOU KNOW?

Nearly half of all the people who live in British Columbia—two million—live in and around Vancouver.

DID YOU KNOW?

Vancouver's Stanley Park is the biggest city park in all of Canada—1,000 acres—and there are squirrels everywhere. That's because nearly one hundred years ago, New York City gave Vancouver eight pairs of gray squirrels, and they just kept making more squirrels.

DID YOU KNOW?

More than twenty million people cross Puget Sound on the Washington State Ferries every year. People commute to work—and sometimes school—on the ferries. They take their cars, bikes, even canoes and kayaks aboard. Some kids have birthday parties on a ferry.

DID YOU KNOW?

The Klondike Gold Rush turned Seattle into a big city, as businesses opened to supply the gold seekers heading to the Yukon. More than 9,000 people and 36,000 tons of gear left Seattle during the first six weeks of the Gold Rush.

DID YOU KNOW?

Seattle was named after Chief Seattle, a Suquamish Indian who lived in the Puget Sound area in the mid-nineteenth century.

in these waters, like the giant Pacific octopus, the biggest octopus in the world. You can walk through the aquarium's Underwater Dome to see Puget Sound from the point of view of a fish. There's a Touch Tank with starfish and other critters. Twenty kinds of starfish live in Puget Sound, including the sunflower star. That one can have up to twenty-four arms!

Have you ever dreamt of being beamed up to a huge space-ship? Seattle's **Space Needle** isn't a real flying saucer, but it sure looks like one—on stilts. The Space Needle was built for the 1962 World's Fair. It's 605 feet high, and from the viewing room at the top you can see the whole city—and the water and mountains that surround it.

The Space Needle is at **Seattle Center,** seventy-four acres that were first developed for the World's Fair and now are packed with places for kids to have fun and maybe learn something while they're at it. Kids love it here. You can take a ride on a monorail or visit the **Pacific Science Center** and the **Children's Museum.** The Science Center is the place to go for hands-on science fun, from robots to lasers to sky shows. The Children's Museum offers a lot of art workshops, among other things. Younger kids like the Fun Forest, a collection of carnival rides and minigolf. Older kids especially like Experience Music Project. You can record your own songs, learn to play the electric guitar, and take a picture that look like you're in a band.

The hard part is picking where to go first!

Money Smarts

Even though you'll understand what people are saying in Vancouver, the city is part of a different country: Canada. That means there's a different government and different money here. Canadians have a prime minister instead of a president, and a House of Commons instead of a House of Representatives. There are senators, but they represent provinces instead of states. Vancouver is a city in the province of British Columbia in the country of Canada.

That's why your parents need to show your passport or birth certificate at the airport when you fly in and out of Vancouver. People from the United States like to shop here because one U.S. dollar is worth more than one Canadian dollar. That means you'll think you're getting a bargain in the stores. The exchange rate changes all the time, though. Can you figure out how much your U.S. money is worth when you visit? The Canadian dollar is a big gold-colored coin that people here call the "Loonie" because it features the Canadian loon on its face. But don't worry if you don't have any Canadian dollars; most Vancouver stores will take U.S. dollars.

Sightseeing Smarts

Big cities like Vancouver and Seattle can be lots of fun—or very boring—for kids. The trick is to figure out where to go and what to do to have the most fun. Of course everyone in the family might not want to do the same things. Web sites like the ones we've listed in this book will help. Look for "just for kids" areas, and you'll soon become the family expert. Tell your mom and dad

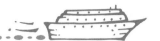

you'd like to be the tour-leader-for-the-day, that way you're guaranteed to have a great time! But be sure to compromise so that everyone gets to see something they want. Everyone will be a lot happier. Don't forget to wear comfortable shoes and stash a windbreaker and some snacks in your backpack. Most important, leave lots of time to enjoy being outdoors.

A Seattle Kid Says

Get a picture of yourself at the Experience Music Project as part of a rock band.

–TAREK, 14

Favorite Place

Draw a picture or write about the most fun place you visited in Seattle or Vancouver. Why did you like it so much?

CHAPTER 11

Saying Good-bye

The cruise can't be over—not yet. It seems like you just boarded the ship!

By now you've made new friends, seen tons of glaciers and maybe a bear or a whale, eaten lots of salmon, and stayed up late every night.

Now it's time to pack—and figure out how to cram all those souvenirs into your suitcase. Where are you going to put that stuffed whale? The totem pole? Even worse, you'll have to pack the night before and put your suitcase outside your cabin before you go to bed so that the crew can get everyone's luggage off the ship in the morning.

You don't want to forget one minute of the trip. Sit down with your friends, a pen, and this book. They will help you to always remember.

New Friends

How many different places are your shipboard friends from?

_____

_____

_____

_____

_____

_____

_____

Don't forget to take a picture of all of you together. Write your friends' addresses here:

_____

_____

_____

_____

_____

_____

_____

_____

_____

_____

_____

_____

_____

_____

_____

_____

_____

_____

Counselors

Counselors helped make the trip fun—especially at night. Got their pictures too? What are their names? Where are they from?

_____

_____

_____

_____

_____

_____

_____

_____

Waiters

Waiters on cruise ships become kids' good friends and bring them everything they want (if mom and dad say yes). Take a picture during your last dinner. What were your waiters' names? Where are they from?

_____

_____

_____

_____

_____

_____

_____

Ha! Ha!
What was the funniest thing that happened to you on the ship?

_____

_____

_____

_____

_____

_____

In Alaska?

_____

_____

_____

_____

Souvenir Smarts
What souvenirs did you buy?

_____

_____

_____

_____

Next Time

If you could come back to Alaska, what would you like to do again?

_____

_____

_____

_____

_____

_____

_____

_____

_____

_____

_____

_____

_____

_____

_____

_____

_____

Appendix

Here are mailing addresses, Web sites, and phone numbers for cities and places in Alaska. This information can help you and your parents track down all you'll need to know to plan your trip.

General Web Sites

www.everythingalaska.com
www.nps.gov/webrangers
www.travelalaska.com

Anchorage

www.anchorage.net

Alaska Native Heritage Center, 8800 Heritage Center Drive, Anchorage, AK 99506; (907) 330–8000; www.alaska native.net

Alaska Public Lands Information Center; 605 West 4th Avenue,
Suite 105, Anchorage, AK 99501; (907) 271–2737; www.nps.gov/aplic/center

Alaska SeaLife Center, 301 Railway Avenue, P.O. Box 1329, Seward, AK 99664; (907) 224–6300; www.alaskasea life.org

Alaska Zoo, 4731 O'Malley Road, Anchorage, AK 99507; (907) 346–1088; www.alaskazoo.org

Anchorage Museum of History and Art, 121 West 7th Avenue, Anchorage, AK 99501; (907) 343–6173; www.anchorage museum.org

H2Oasis Indoor Waterpark, 1520 O'Malley Road, Anchorage, AK 99507; (907) 522–4420; www.h2oasiswater park.com

Iditarod, P.O. Box 870800, Wasilla, AK 99687; (907) 376–5155; www.iditarod .com

Imaginarium Science Center, 737 West 5th Avenue, Suite G, Anchorage, AK 99501; (907) 276–3179; www.imagin arium.org

Denali National Park

Denali National Park, P.O. Box 9, Denali Park, AK 99755; (907) 683–2294; www.denalinationalpark.com

Juneau

www.traveljuneau.com

Alaska State Museum, 395 Whittier Street, Juneau, AK 99801–1718; (907) 465–2901; www.museums.state.ak.us

Macaulay Salmon Hatchery, 2697 Channel Drive, Juneau, AK 99801; (907) 463–5114; www.dipac.net

Mendenhall Glacier Visitor Center, 8465 Old Dairy Road, Juneau, AK 99801; (907) 789–0097; www.fs.fed.us/r10/ tongass/districts/mendenhall

Ketchikan

www.visit-Ketchikan.com

Deer Mountain Tribal Hatchery & Eagle Center, 1158 Salmon Road, Ketchikan, AK 99901; (907) 225–6761; kictribe.org/ Hatchery

Great Alaskan Lumberjack Show, P.O. Box 23343, Ketchikan, AK 99901, (907) 247–9050; www.lumberjacksports.com

Totem Heritage Center, 601 Deermont Street, Ketchikan, AK 99901; (907) 225–5900

Petersburg

www.petersburg.org

Seattle

www.seeseattle.org

Children's Museum, 305 Harrison Street, Seattle, WA 98109; (206) 441–1768; www.thechildrensmuseum.org

Experience Music Project, 325 5th Avenue North, Seattle, WA 98109; (206) 367–5483; www.emplive.com

Pacific Science Center, 200 Second Avenue North, Seattle, WA 98109; (206) 443–2001; www.pacsci.org

Pike Place Market; (206) 682–7453; www.pikeplacemarket.org

Seattle Art Museum, 100 University Street, Seattle, WA 98101–2902; (206) 654–3100; www.seattleartmuseum.org

Seattle Aquarium, Pier 59, 1483 Alaskan Way, Seattle, WA 98101; (206) 386–4300; www.seattleaquarium.org

Seattle Center; (206) 684–7200; www.seattlecenter.com

Space Needle, 400 Broad Street, Seattle, WA 98109; (206) 905–2100; www.space-needle.com

Sitka

www.sitka.com

Alaska Raptor Center, 1000 Raptor Way, Sitka, AK 99835; (907) 747–8662; www.alaskaraptor.org

St. Michael's Cathedral, Lincoln Street, P.O. Box 697, Sitka, AK 99835; (907) 747–8120

Skagway

www.skagway.org

Klondike Gold Rush National Historic Park, Second and Broadway, P.O. Box 517, Skagway, AK 99840; (907) 983–2921; www.nps.gov/klgo

White Pass and Yukon Route Railroad, P.O. Box 435, Skagway, AK 99840; (907) 983–2217; www.whitepassrailroad .com

Vancouver

www.tourismvancouver.com

Capilano Suspension Bridge and Park, 3735 Capilano Road, North Vancouver, British Columbia, Canada VTR 4J1; (604) 985–7474; www.capbridge.com

Gastown, at Hastings Street and Water Street, Vancouver, British Columbia, Canada V6B 2K7; (604) 683–5650; www.gastown.org

Granville Island, 1661 Duranleau Street, Vancouver, British Columbia, Canada V6H 3S3; (604) 666–6655; www.granvilleisland.bc.ca

Stanley Park; (604) 257–8400; www.city.vancouver.bc.ca/parks/parks& gardens/stanley.htm

University of British Columbia Museum of Anthropology, 6393 NW Marine Drive, Vancouver, British Columbia, Canada V6T 1Z2; (604) 822–5087; www.moa.ubc.ca

Vancouver Aquarium, P.O. Box 3232, Vancouver, British Columbia, Canada V6B 3X8; (604) 659–3474; www.vanaqua.org

Vancouver Museum, 1100 Chestnut Street, Vancouver, British Columbia, Canada V6J 3J9; (604) 736–4431; www.vanmuseum.bc.ca

Wrangell

www.wrangell.com